MW00640558

48 LAWS

OF

FORECLOSURE
DEFENSE

ANTHONY MARTINEZ

Printed in the United States of America.

ISBN: 9781661429225 (E-Book)
ISBN: 9781647865092 (Hardcover)
ISBN: 9781647865115 (Paperback)

LEGAL DISCLAIMER

All of the information found in this book, is based upon the professional and personal experiences of the Author as it applies to foreclosure litigation related matters. While you as the reader may identify with what is written in this book, that information should not, nor any of the information contained in the book, be construed as legal advice.

Legal information is not legal advice. A lawsuit is a serious matter. If you require specific legal advice, you should always consult a licensed practicing attorney in your state.

To my wife Teresa, my sons Anthony and Michael and my daughters Kali, Amaya and Jenelle.

Love you! - Dad

ACKNOWLEGMENTS

First, I would like to thank God for giving me this incredible life.

I would also like to thank my beautiful wife Teresa Martinez and my gifted kids Anthony, Michael, Kali, Amaya and Jenelle for being my reason and air. Because what's life without air.

I've worked with some incredible attorneys over the past 13 years. Too many to name. I thank you all and will see you all throughout the seminars across the country. Many of you have and will continue to be great panelist. Together, we will continue to educate attorneys and the people.

I would especially like to thank my closest attorneys and friends. Tom, you are an incredible attorney and friend who should run for office (pick an office, any office and you will win!). Your friendship and work relationship helped me become one of the best amongst the best (remember that 3rd DCA oral argument... HAHAHAHA – AWESOME!). You are awesome in every way so don't let anyone ever tell you different!

I would also like to thank Niles. You've given me the room and confidence to help set precedence and redefine foreclosure defense strategies and tactics. You should run for President of your State Bar. Not only are you qualified and capable, you're likely one of the very few that can make the Bar the organization it needs to be. The future is bright for you and I will always be there when you need me (especially if you become President of the Bar because I would gladly be your chief investigator to put all this unlawful foreclosure fraud to bed).

This thank you list will go on forever so I would also like to thank all the trial attorneys I've worked with and those I didn't, whose work I admired over the past ten years to help families save their homes from unlawful foreclosure. Mark, Matt, Evan, Bruce and Kelley are legends in their own right who fought the crucial issues and helped create some of the best caselaw in foreclosure.

I'd like to thank all of the judges across the country who have ruled good and bad. We can't have the sweet without the sour. You have all made a better man out of me, a loving man of humanity that humbly and graciously remains the tip of the sword for those who cannot defend themselves. If only we could all remain impartial and adjudicate every matter on the merits.

Lastly and most importantly, I'd like to thank every American who has fought against the fraud to keep the American Dream of homeownership and family alive. To all of you, God Bless! Only your vote can change the wrong in America.

"Either write something worth reading or do something worth writing."

— **Benjamin Franklin**

CONTENTS

PREFACE

In 2008 the housing and financial markets crashed causing most of America to go into foreclosure. What many people didn't know was that their loan origination itself, was a sham, a fraud that was silently committed by organized fraudsters. The scheme began wherein ABC Mortgage Company or Bank, was named as the lender on your Note and Mortgage but wasn't the party that actually funded the loan. Instead, they were middlemen, playing a part for a hefty commission, all the while keeping the actual funding source – the real creditor to whom the debt was owed, invisible.

The 2008 housing market crash wasn't some fluke anomaly, it was the greatest robbery in history. It was a robbery worth well over 11 trillion dollars, and we were the victims. Too big to fail? That was Wall Street's way of saying we are the real La Cosa Nostra in America. Lawsuits for fraud by investors and the Attorney General's for each of the states, against the banks? Who cares! What's a few hundred billion in fines and settlements when you just took the country for over $11 trillion? The housing market crash was no fluke, it was the largest robbery in American history.

Americans lost more than their homes. America watched the American dream of owning a home, having a family, kids growing up and leaving to college, the dog and the white picket fence dream, that American dream... was extinguished. They destroyed many families. Husbands and wives divorced. Children lost the safety of their bedrooms and lost their friends. The elderly lost their lifetime homes, and many watched their significant others die while some, committed suicide. Wall Street destroyed the American Dream in this robbery, and no one went to jail.

For the lawyers, foreclosure became a new practice area of law. When the 2008 foreclosure crisis emerged, there was very little foreclosure related case law on the books. If there was case law, it was straight forward and didn't deal with multi-deal complex contracts like those found in securitization of loans. The foreclosure law on the books, at the time of the market crash, was no match for what this foreclosure wave would bring. Foreclosure case law was nonapplicable and statutes on the books across every state, had to be updated and changed. After the 2008 crash, every foreclosure case presented potential new case law. Even attorneys with 20 and 30 years of real estate experience, had no clue how to defend a foreclosure case. Judges across America knew nothing. Why? Because foreclosure, after the housing market crash, was not conventional at all. Maybe on the outer shell it looks like a normal, arm's length transaction but its foundation was deep rooted in undisclosed deals. The courts were unaware of the complexities of the origination of these loans. It was not as simple as, you took a loan, you stopped making payments, so the bank foreclosed. Judges had the mindset that banks are in the business of lending money so if they say you owe, I'm sure you do.

The truth was, these loans being foreclosed on, they weren't just arms-length transactions that involved a note and mortgage, that was just where the coverup and fraudulent behavior began. I mean, didn't anyone feel just a little suspicious that their credit score was in the 500's yet they were being approved for a $500,000.00 home? These loans being foreclosed on, were complex contracts that involved layers of other transactional contracts that were never disclosed to the borrowers and were deliberately hidden by the banks. Judges on Wall Street at 60 Centre Street in New York, are well versed in complex contract litigation matters involving these Wall Street banks right around the corner, but a Judge in Lee Country Florida? Nahhh! Judges across America had no clue that these foreclosure cases were, in fact, complex contract litigation matters with a deep core of omittance of facts that could render each loan transaction, void.

These loans were "supposed to" act as investment securities referred to as Mortgage-Backed Securities (MBS) but it was all a lie. It was a lie because banks would present a proposal to potential investors called a Prospectus, that said hey, we have pooled together a thousand prime rate residential mortgages that value $2 billion and will yield say $10 Billion in profit. These investors varied. Some were pension funds and other retirement type funds. So, these MBS's affected Americans directly if they failed. But here is what the banks failed to disclose to these investors… they didn't have the loans yet. The lie was, the banks did already have possession of the loans the investors were investing in. Instead, they were taking investor funds to finance the whole acquisition operation and made warehouse lines of credit available to originators. Warehouse funding is where an ABC Mortgage Company or bank would secure a loan, claim they were the lender that was funding the transaction but, funded the loan through this warehouse line of credit instead. The loan would be funded and the so-called lender (middleman that lied), would receive their commission. In turn, the note and mortgage were supposed to be endorsed and transferred to the real funding source, who in turn, would transfer the note and mortgage to a party called a Depositor for the purported trust that was going to house these loans. The Depositor would then transfer the notes and mortgage into the purported Trust. This is a brief, general version of the process referred to as securitization.

Unfortunately, what I have just described is a ton of paper moving around, lots of FedExing and too much room for human error. How can this manual process work with the electronic transfer of money that moved a thousand times faster? It couldn't. So, the banks came up with Mortgage Electronic Registration Systems ("MERS"), an electronic registration system that would digitize the loan closings and allow the documents to move electronically with the money. Makes sense, right? Wrong! In theory it made sense until they tried to foreclose, and the Judge said, "hey dude, where's the original note?" That's right, you must be in possession of and must produce to the court, the original wet ink note, if you want to foreclose. Well holy shit Batman, where are the millions of original notes? DESTROYED!!! At least that's what the Florida Banking Association confessed to the Florida Supreme Court.

For MERS to work, original documents were scanned and then destroyed. But if they were only scanned at the origination stage and then destroyed, how did the multiple "required" endorsements get on the so-called original note from the originator to the real funding source, to the depositor and then in blank or specific to the purported trust? The short answer is, they were destroyed, so new originals had to be created and most times the so-called original presented to the court, was either a high-quality color copy or a reconstructed original. This was accomplished by taking a copy of a borrower's signature and recreating it with an arm pen – a device that effectively aces the recreation of a signature and re-signs it with original ink making it look like an exact original. How's that for criminal enterprise? You didn't think the blue ink pen wasn't for a specific reason, did you?

Sounds messy, doesn't it? Well, the truth is, these original loans never made it through the process they were intended for. Investors were lied to, borrowers were lied to, and the courts were lied to. All for the American religion of capitalism. The government flooded the streets of America with deadly drugs for capitalism. Drug dealers sell illegal drugs on street corners in the name of capitalism. Doctors prescribe opioids for a commission on every pill for the love of capitalism. Banks will engage in financial crimes for the love of capitalism. Lawyers will over bill clients in the name of capitalism and judges, our last line of defense, will close a blind eye to our cries. Sell us all out for that raise and the security of their investments and pensions, all for the love of capitalism!

Twelve years later, we are now in 2020 and foreclosure is not only alive and well, business is BOOMING! Foreclosure is now a new business model for fraudster companies, falsely claiming to be the "servicer" of the loan. Like bottom feeder credit card companies who paid pennies on the dollar for discharged debts paid off by insurance claims, these servicers now unlawfully foreclose under the same premise with a twist. They foreclose in the name of another to hide themselves, but they are the opposing force. They are the ones that hire the foreclosure mill law firms to file these unlawful foreclosures. They are the ones now seeking to steal your home and do so with impunity. For them, it's about the sale of your property and the recovery of hundreds of thousands of dollars in profit for the pennies they put out. For the foreclosure mill lawyers, they've sold their souls for the dollar. They have gladly violated their oaths as officers of the court. They file these fraudulent actions riddled with misrepresentations, on behalf of these servicers, in the name of someone other than the name of the party that hired them, with no remorse for the outcome. These servicers and foreclosure mill law firms commit these crimes because the judiciary, our last line of defense, has allowed them to.

Foreclosure, in 2020, represents the second wave of a new financial crisis. The difference between this new foreclosure epidemic and the 2008 one is that this time, we are armed with knowledge, information, resources, experience and are overall, better prepared. Many of the courts are under a greater scrutiny today than they were yesterday. Some exposed in corruption while others, forced to submit to the truth thanks to pro-se fighters and attorney's that sacrificed themselves to pierce their armor. Many maintained blogs over the years and some wrote books.

Regardless of your personal views or political positions, one thing is for certain, remaining neutral is no longer an option. You are either part of the solution or you're part of the problem. History will determine who was on the right side of this fight and who was on the wrong side. The American Dream doesn't begin with capitalism. It begins with love. A love that is housed in a home amongst family. You might not believe the 2020 foreclosure epidemic affects you, but it does.

Do a brief investigation on what the divorce rate in America was pre 2008 and post 2008, to present. Talk to millennials about their views on having children. Home ownership is bigger than the house you buy or what you paid for it. Homeownership is one of the biggest parts of the American Dream and it affects us all!

WHAT THIS BOOK IS ABOUT

This book is an awakening. These are not 48 statutes (laws) from around the country related to foreclosure. I am giving you 48 important things you should be consciously aware of, when you face foreclosure.

Whether you realize it or not, refuse to accept it or not, the foreclosure you are engaged in, is likely an unlawful foreclosure. If you are a homeowner, you are probably a victim of it. If you are a defense attorney, you need to wake up about it. Unlawful foreclosure is a business model.

These 48 Laws are based on my national case and courtroom experience. Foreclosure defense attorneys are predominantly local which means, their arguments and litigation style are based on what they see and how the judge's rule in that local court. If you have 3 local judges and all 3 judges are pro-bank, who will change their minds?

1ˢᵀ LAW
OF
FORECLOSURE
DEFENSE

FORECLOSURE DEFENSE

LAW

1

The Quiet Before the Foreclosure Storm and the Claim of Default

Most, if not all foreclosure filings, are predicated on a claim of default. This is when there has been a claim of non-payment of the monthly installment payment due. When there is a claim of non-payment default, it constitutes a breach of the contract. In most cases, if you miss three (3) payments, the party you've been making your payment to, will send you a letter saying you are in default and they are turning this matter over to their legal counsel to start foreclosure proceedings against you. This is the quiet before the foreclosure storm. It is the period between a series of scary letters that make you feel like they are coming to take your house and the actual knock on the door by a sheriff or process server who serves you with the foreclosure lawsuit papers filed against you in court.

If this is your first foreclosure, then study this book. Over 90% of all alleged defaults are false and/or misleading for a series of reasons. This includes the wrong amounts claimed in the default. Commonly those amounts are the product of multiple refusals to accept your monthly payment and the false claim that your payments have not been received. It's also 2020, so for many, any foreclosure filing is likely a refiling premised on a new claim of default on a loan modification or a new claim of default after a previous case was dismissed. No matter the reason, it is probable the foreclosure is the product of a misleading default claim. So, get ready, because the fraud is real, and it's headed right for you. If you are in the quiet before the foreclosure storm, don't wait to be served before you prepare, begin the moment they make you aware that a foreclosure will be filed against you.

2ND LAW
OF
FORECLOSURE
DEFENSE

FORECLOSURE DEFENSE
LAW
2

Your Guilt Doesn't Justify Their Fraud

Maybe you stopped making your payments for a number of reasons. You may have stopped making your payments because your Servicer or Lender told you that to qualify for a loan modification you had to be in default first, before they could help you modify your payments. Maybe you stopped making your payments because they put forced placed insurance that raised your monthly payment amount. You could have been making your payments but for nefarious reasons that were not yours, the Servicer or Lender may have stopped accepting your payments because they intended to foreclose no matter what. Sometimes people stop making

5

payments because the adjustable rate in their note increased the monthly payment. Maybe you stopped making payments because you couldn't afford the payment anymore regardless of the amount.

Always remember that has nothing to do with the possibility that the person you've paid, couldn't demand, accept and keep your monthly payments. It also doesn't change the reality that they likely filed in public records, misleading and fraudulent documents to create a false entitlement to take your money and have a lien interest in your property.

To prevail in successful foreclosure defense, it will require that you put the illusional, often, self-inflicted guilt you feel because of a non-payment, to the side. Just because a foreclosure is filed against you, doesn't mean you should convince yourself that it's warranted. Experience had taught the greatest foreclosure defense lawyers and pro-se litigants to understand and realize that most foreclosures filed, are by parties who do not have standing to sue but use the law and bias of the courts to steal your property.

3RD LAW
OF
FORECLOSURE
DEFENSE

FORECLOSURE DEFENSE

LAW

3

Understanding the Foreclosure Matrix

In 2008 the housing market crashed. Here we are in 2020 and the foreclosure crisis still exists. While there may not be as many foreclosure filings like the gold rush in 2008 and 2009, there are just as many defaults occurring because of the adjustable rate explosions, bogus loan modification defaults and foreclosure as a new business model for deceptive loan servicers. Understanding the foreclosure matrix means understanding that foreclosure is like a spider's web, once you're caught in it, it's very difficult to get out of. You may get your foreclosure case dismissed, but they will refile because the law across the land allows these fraudsters to refile as many times as they want until they finally foreclose, leaving you stuck in the web.

The key to great foreclosure defensive and offensive strategy is figuring out how to remove yourself from the foreclosure web and still be able to fight the good fight against the fraud and hold the fraudsters accountable. You should not try to do this in foreclosure defense. Do this apart from the defense of the foreclosure action in a counterclaim or separate action for damages if it's not compulsory which means it *has to be done* as a counterclaim in the foreclosure action.

Many pro-se litigants and defense attorneys make the mistake of not understanding actual foreclosure practice versus foreclosure theories. As you engage in foreclosure defense, always remember that the facts and not the theories, are what will allow you to prevail.

4TH LAW OF FORECLOSURE DEFENSE

FORECLOSURE DEFENSE
LAW
4

The Lawsuit Has Been Filed Against You, Don't Panic You Have Options

There is no greater intimidation tactic than that "KNOCK - KNOCK" from the process server or the sheriff to serve you with the foreclosure summons and complaint. It's a moment where you become scared, anxiety may rush in, you believe the foreclosure process is fast and you have days left to stay in your home. This isn't the case, so take a step back and breathe.

You are not the first person served with a foreclosure action and you will not be the last. You have resources at your disposal. Some free and some that will cost you. Don't make the mistake of a knee jerk reaction that causes you to waive your rights to defend yourself. Like a magic trick, you're likely being played and there's an illusion taking place in front of you, the facts of which you are not yet aware of.

There is a fact-finding mission that you will need to go on and this will take some time. Prepare to be patient, be willing and be diligent. Slow down and don't be so quick to react. Whether you know it or even want to believe it, there is a high probability the foreclosure filed against you is unlawful and until you can decipher the truth, don't be in a rush to waive your ability to defend yourself. Always remember you should admit nothing and deny everything! Not knowing what to do means you need to find a lawyer quickly.

5TH LAW OF FORECLOSURE DEFENSE

FORECLOSURE DEFENSE LAW 5

You've Been Served Start the 20/30 Day Clock to Respond

Ok, you got the knock on the door and they have served you with the lawsuit. Take a breath, calm down and relax. First and far most, clock your calendar 20/30 days (depending on your jurisdiction) which runs the next day after they have served you and set a reminder alert at least 5 days in advance that a response to the complaint is due in case you lose track of time. A proactive foreclosure mill firm will move to default you on day 21/31 so, you have to be diligent. If you will not represent yourself pro-se and have a hard time finding competent counsel to represent you, file the response yourself.

If you don't know what you're doing, file an extension of time to respond. You can do this by writing a letter or drafting a formal motion. This will give you more time to find a lawyer and respond to the complaint. It also avoids the entry of a default against you. Often, the motion or letter for more time to the court says you have been trying to find good defense counsel but could not. This letter or motion requests from the court at least 30 more days from the entry of the court order, to give you more time to file a response to the complaint. Do not make the mistake of letting the service time of 20/30 go by. The entry of default waives your right to defend and allows all the allegations in the complaint to stand as true. If they enter a default against you, the foreclosure mill firm will move for summary judgment, conduct a sale, seek title and then take possession of your home.

6TH LAW
OF
FORECLOSURE
DEFENSE

FORECLOSURE DEFENSE
LAW
6

This is a Civil Case But Remember Anything You Say or Do Can and Will Be Used Against You

In a criminal case, after an arrest, they must read the accused their Miranda Rights. This doesn't apply to civil cases but in an abundance of caution, practice the reality of Miranda in that anything you say or do can and will be used against you in a court of law.

Now that they have served you with the lawsuit, your first instinct may be to write to the court and tell them how you lost your job and cannot afford the payments. You might also try to explain to the court that you stopped making the payments for a specific reason other than unaffordability. Either way, placing a confession on paper guarantees that it will be use against you as an admission. You have rights and legal defenses at your disposal. Always hire a good foreclosure defense attorney and not just any attorney, to help you protect yourself and your rights. Don't try to represent yourself pro-se if you don't have to.

Foreclosure mill firms riddle complaints with deception, misleading information and statements designed to mislead the court. At every turn, they will try to tap into the bias of the court to frame you as a deadbeat who has been living in the property for free in an effort to take your home away from you. Say nothing and don't do anything that may contribute to the loss of your home without first knowing and understanding all available options.

7TH LAW
OF
FORECLOSURE
DEFENSE

FORECLOSURE DEFENSE LAW

7

Who is Really Filing the Foreclosure Against You?

In foreclosure, understanding and asking the questions, "who, what, when, where and why", are important if you want to stop this robbery in progress. You'll find that asking why is the most critical. For example, why is the party named as the Plaintiff in the foreclosure not the party that hired the law firm to file the foreclosure action against you?

The hiring party is an entity likely claiming to be the servicer of the loan. Why is a company that possibly never collected payments, buying the servicing rights (if they did at all) to a non-performing loan to file a foreclosure in someone else's name? Who is this so-called servicer, making insurance mortgage payments and paying the taxes on the property despite not being in a contractual relationship with you? Why are they making monthly distribution payments to the investors but claiming to the court the loan is non-performing due to a default? What else are they paying on your behalf and why?

Make no mistake, who, what, when and how are very important questions that will need answers but, understanding why, is a priority to understanding the foreclosure action filed against you. Always remember that someone willing and with the means to pay tens of thousands of dollars to receive hundreds of thousands of dollars in return, will gladly take the chance to steal your home.

8TH LAW
OF
FORECLOSURE
DEFENSE

FORECLOSURE DEFENSE

LAW

8

Investors, Lenders and Servicers – Who is Who?

It is important that you not confuse the players in this foreclosure. Investors are the parties that put up the money to finance your loan. A Lender is the party that funded your loan. A Servicer, is the party the lender hired to service your loan by collecting the monthly payments, communicating with you about your loan or changes thereto and the party responsible for making third-party payments. These third-party payments refer to taxes, insurance, distribution payments to investors and other miscellaneous payments related to your loan. Often, servicers sell their servicing rights to other companies who then become the new servicer of your loan.

Here's the thing though, if Investors are the parties responsible for funding your loan, doesn't that make them the actual lender? Why weren't they disclosed at your closing if real estate loans are transparent and arm's length transactions? If the Investor is the real financing party, why is someone else named as the Lender on the Note and Mortgage if they're not the funding source? Did the lender identified on the Note and Mortgage receive a commission to play the middleman and hide the identity of the real funding source? Lastly, if the so-called Servicer works for the named Lender but the named Lender isn't the Lender, is the Servicer entitled to demand and collect your monthly mortgage payments?

Foreclosure is not as simple as we make them out to be. They connect the parties involved through a series of other very complex contracts that may affect your case.

9TH LAW

9TH LAW
OF
FORECLOSURE
DEFENSE

FORECLOSURE DEFENSE LAW

9

The Servicer is Not the Owner of Your Loan

Sometimes a bank or finance company that owns your loan is also the servicer of the loan. However, in most foreclosure cases, the lender and servicer are two different parties and it is the servicer that has hired the foreclosure mill law firm to file the foreclosure action against you. Thus, often, the servicer of your loan is not the owner of your loan.

More often than not, the servicer is not the named Plaintiff in the case against you. So, where you may be familiar with a servicing company that you receive letters or statements from each month, as the party you were making your monthly mortgage payments to, it may confuse you to see a different bank or company being named as the Plaintiff in the foreclosure filed against you.

When a foreclosure is filed against you, it's common they name the Investor as the Plaintiff. For the first time, during the loan's life; you finally get to see who they are. Knowing "who" all the players are and their exact roles are critical to identifying misleading statements in your foreclosure so pay close attention and make a note every time a new name pops up in your case.

10TH LAW OF FORECLOSURE DEFENSE

FORECLOSURE DEFENSE
LAW
10

Servicing Fraud Translates Into Unlawful Foreclosure

Like credit card bottom feeders who purchase credit card debt for pennies on the dollar, so-called "servicers" are no different. Consider what a bottom feeder is; one who purchases debt after the charge off of the debt and insurance has paid the debt off. Using credit card bottom feeders as an example, they purchase the credit card debt for pennies on the dollar. They then contact you and offer to cut your debt in half today if you make a partial or full payment to reset the statute of limitations clock.

In the same context, they sell servicing rights on what we call "non-performing loans". These "Servicers" who have claimed to purchase the servicing rights, go in for the foreclosure kill lying to the court that they've been damaged by your non-payment and need to sell your property to recover their loss. In that same way, these fraudsters will offer you a loan modification at a lower APR over 30 years. You may think it a good deal but what they are doing is attempting to create new legal documents to cure the defective unenforceable ones just like credit card bottom feeders do. This is the new foundation for Unlawful Foreclosure in 2020.

11TH LAW
OF
FORECLOSURE
DEFENSE

FORECLOSURE DEFENSE

LAW

11

Filing False, Misleading & Fraudulent Documents in Public Records

Often, without your knowledge because there is no requirement to provide you with notice, those who foreclose on your property, set into motion, the ability to validate their false claim of entitlement to foreclose your home. One of the number of ways they do this is by filing a fraudulent Assignment of Mortgage (AOM) in public records.

An AOM is a document that memorializes the transfer of the mortgage but often transfers the mortgage "together with the note." Sometimes these AOM's are legitimate, however, they are often riddled with misleading information. Courts rely on these false documents throughout the lawsuit.

In most states, filing a false document in public records is a crime. State statutes provide civil remedies for criminal acts so check your state laws to confirm the criminal act of filing false documents in public records has a civil remedy. These false document filings can become damage claims in a counterclaim or separate action for damages.

12TH LAW OF FORECLOSURE DEFENSE

FORECLOSURE DEFENSE
LAW
12

Don't Let the Foreclosure Mill Law Firms Fool You

A lawsuit filed against you is serious business. A foreclosure is an attempt to take your property away from you to satisfy a debt owed. Having these legal papers filed and served on you is intimidating and if you don't have a lawyer, you can become the victim of severe anxiety, emotional distress and physically illness caused by stress.

Foreclosure mill law firms file template style complaints tailored to your loan information. They're "mills" because they pump out these lawsuits as a matter of course. They rely on the fact that most foreclosures go undefended. This allows for a default entered against the homeowner and the entry of a final judgment. After they secure judgment, they move to sell the property and secure title. They then seek eviction against you if you still maintain possession of the property.

Consider that a lawyer willing to file a misleading or fraudulent based lawsuit to steal your property and remove your children or your elderly parents from their home for profit, is a dangerous adversary. Don't let them fool you. They don't want to help you; they only want to win. Consider this reality every time you communicate with them or any time you are in court with them. Always remember the practice of law is an adversarial process. They are not your friend. They represent the party trying to take your property, sell it and kick you out.

13TH LAW OF FORECLOSURE DEFENSE

FORECLOSURE DEFENSE
LAW
13

Foreclosure is Capitalism and Capitalism Breeds Dishonesty

You better believe that even though lawyers take oaths and are officers of the court, many will lie and cheat in court for money. Foreclosure is about money. Companies are in the business of making money and foreclosure mill law firms are in the business of helping those companies make their money by manipulating the law in their favor and against you so that they can get paid too.

A home loan is for hundreds of thousands of dollars and is probably the largest personal loan you will ever receive. A foreclosure is the process by which a party and their lawyers are taking legal steps to take that home from you and sell it to get paid hundreds of thousands of dollars. It may seem logical that a party who has lent you hundreds of thousands of dollars may sell the property to get it back. But what is the logic of a party who didn't fund the loan or purchased the loan at value, to file an unlawful foreclosure to steal the property to sell it?

Foreclosure is complex, and it is imperative that you hold a foreclosing party's feet to the fire to determine if the party foreclosing may do so. Their vision of capitalism involves fraud and conspiracy to defraud. There is no such thing as a billionaire who didn't commit a crime to get there and foreclosure is a trillion-dollar industry.

14TH LAW OF FORECLOSURE DEFENSE

FORECLOSURE DEFENSE
LAW
14

Never Represent Yourself if You Don't Have To

There is a saying amongst lawyers - a lawyer who represents himself is a fool. If you can afford a lawyer, hire one. Foreclosure is like a divorce because it is filled with emotion and is draining. It is an uphill battle against a multi-trillion-dollar industry and a judge that's likely pro-bank and who assumes you're a deadbeat trying to get a free house.

A foreclosure is for hundreds of thousands of dollars, the largest personal loan you've ever had. Don't go into this fight thinking you will spend a few hundred or a few thousand dollars fighting a trillion-dollar industry. Be strategic in the way you move to defend yourself and your property. Be cognizant of the reality that wars cost money so, create a war chest. Treat your foreclosure case like it's a war because it is. Someone has declared war against you to deprive you of your constitutional right to your property and happiness. Defend yourself.

The people who have declared war against you, don't care about your spouse. They don't care about your children and don't they care about your health. Do not make the mistake of thinking they want to help you. Capitalism mandates they first seek to help themselves.

15TH LAW OF FORECLOSURE DEFENSE

FORECLOSURE DEFENSE
LAW
15

You Can't Represent Yourself if You Don't Have the Gift of Gab

90% of every decision a judge makes in foreclosure cases will be in an oral argument on a motion scheduled for hearing in front of them. That means you have to be a good speaker who can articulate thoughts and respond on the fly. That's what a good litigator does.

A good litigator is like a salesman and a good salesman can sell anyone anything. It's the proverbial make them believe sand is water. You will need to sell the judge on your argument and why the judge should rule in your favor.

Consider that judges do not believe you are a victim. They believe you want a house for free. Keep in mind that judges believe the fraudsters over you. Judges have bias against you as a homeowner and will rule against you when given the opportunity. Do not make the mistake of assuming the judge will be fair.

Now consider your personality and ask yourself if the court will take to you. Ask yourself if your personality can sway a judge to listen to what you have to say. If all you think you have to do is pretend to be a lawyer and talk like one, you are sure to lose. Litigators are fluent in the rules of civil procedure and the rules of evidence. They know when and how to quote them. It's all a part of their courtroom spiel that is artfully interwoven with their passion and gift of gab.

16TH LAW
OF
FORECLOSURE
DEFENSE

FORECLOSURE DEFENSE LAW

16

Remaining Pro-Se is Dangerous and Not Advisable

It's one thing to start off Pro-Se because of time running out to respond to a complaint, do something that's needed or lack of funds at the time they filed the foreclosure. Do what you have to do to survive but work forward not remaining Pro-Se.

The courtroom is like a club where they speak their own language. You're not part of the club and most judges are not fond of Pro-Se Defendants or Petitioners because they are not familiar with the rules of procedure and motion practice. Judges feel Pro-Se people waste the court's time.

Representing yourself already puts you at a disadvantage. If you represent yourself, the judge will not help you and is obligated to treat you just like an attorney. They will hold you to the same standard as an attorney. Many Pro-Se people hurt foreclosure case law as do bad attorneys who don't know how to properly defend a foreclosure case.

Consider that you don't have a law degree or the courtroom experience of a trained and seasoned attorney so, take representing yourself serious.

17TH LAW OF FORECLOSURE DEFENSE

FORECLOSURE DEFENSE
LAW
17

Not Every Lawyer is a Good Lawyer and Not Every Good Lawyer is a Litigator

Hiring a good foreclosure attorney is a very difficult task. In my experience, there are three kinds of lawyers - writers, researchers and litigators. Remember, 90% of a foreclosure fighter's win-or-lose record will happen in the courtroom in oral arguments. If you can't represent yourself because you don't have the gift of gab, don't believe for one second that a lawyer who doesn't have the gift of gab will do any better.

Knowing the law, rules and procedures is important, but if your lawyer is a stuttering introvert, you are not only wasting your money, you're guaranteeing your demise and loss of your home.

Many judges don't read pleadings before hearings so a good researcher or writer may preserve an issue in writing but lose in court arguing it. A good foreclosure defense lawyer is one who's a talented litigator capable of selling a judge back his own shoes. Like a great salesman, a great litigator will always have the judge saying yes and will walk out of the courtroom with a favorable decision.

18TH LAW OF FORECLOSURE DEFENSE

FORECLOSURE DEFENSE LAW

18

Learn, Learn and Learn Some More

An educated client is a smart client. Not because you're trying to be a lawyer but because the law is a language. If you visit a foreign country, you will learn the language for several reasons, but the most important reason should be, so you're not taken advantage of.

The same applies to your lawyer and the language of law. If you learn the language, then you will be in a better position to not only understand what your lawyer is telling you but be able to ask him the right questions. The most successful foreclosure defense lawyer-client relationship is one where the client understood what was going on in the foreclosure and could take part by maintaining a good relationship and communication dialogue with their attorney.

It is important to understand not only what your lawyer is doing, but what your lawyer is not doing or should be doing. Make Google Scholar one of your favorite resources by searching "foreclosure" under case law. Read and learn how arguments are failing and succeeding in your county, throughout the state and across the country. See what arguments judges seem to be hanging their hat on, see where judges are stagnant and see where judges are flat out failing as a judiciary.

19TH LAW
OF
FORECLOSURE
DEFENSE

FORECLOSURE DEFENSE

LAW

19

Don't Believe Everything You Read on the Internet

This is the biggest problem people encounter when trying to educate themselves on foreclosure. There are a ton of conspiracies related to foreclosure. I call them conspiracies for your own protection. Many of these foreclosure conspiracies may very well be true but most are flawed and almost all of them will do you no good in your case.

If you're reading off the Internet, stick to the blogs and people that have been doing this since the housing market crash in 2008. Foreclosure origins involve very complex financial and contract matters. The same way the law is like a language. So is finance. Don't get caught up on the reality that all the players are criminal minded or criminals.

Stick to the facts of your case and your case only. Citing general nationwide conspiracies of bank fraud and bailouts won't help you or your case. You will find yourself frustrated and losing. If you follow several laws found in this book, you will find yourself in a much better position than flying blind.

20TH LAW OF FORECLOSURE DEFENSE

FORECLOSURE DEFENSE

LAW

20

Know the Life of Your Loan from Inception Forward

They riddled most loans originated before 2008 with false information. The funding was a lie between parties you never met or knew about, for a loan where the lender identified, likely never lent you a dime but received a heavy commission to keep the real parties to the transaction hidden. That's where the complexity of securitized loans begins.

Not knowing the life of the loan is one of the most critical mistakes both lawyers and pro-se defendants make in a foreclosure action.

In your foreclosure case, you will see fabricated assignments of mortgages and endorsements on the note created to foreclose. These endorsements still do not identify the true parties to the loan transaction. Without this information, lies about loan ownerships and rights to enforce will resonate to your detriment. That includes misleading and fraudulent assignments of mortgages recorded in public records to commit a fraud upon the public, you and the court.

21ST LAW
OF
FORECLOSURE
DEFENSE

FORECLOSURE DEFENSE LAW

21

Make Sure the Attorney You Choose Actually Practices Foreclosure Defense and Has Handled Multiple Trials

Any lawyer who says they practice traffic tickets, immigration, dog bites and oh yeah, we do foreclosure too, is not the right lawyer for you. If you speak with a foreclosure defense lawyer who speaks like they work for the bank or seems to always suggest you should give up your home, doesn't know how to defend a foreclosure case. They will only take your money and delay the loss of your home.

A lawyer worth their weight in gold who still uses AOL, MSN or Live as their main work email address, is symbolic of the likelihood they won't understand the complexities of securitization and real foreclosure defense. I would even go so far as to take caution with attorney's that use Gmail, Yahoo or any other free email address as their primary work address. Don't fall for the unfit personal trainer who says he will help you achieve your goals if you pay him to. A real foreclosure defense attorney speaks foreclosure defense as if it's their native tongue.

If you're a foreclosure defense attorney that fits this description, change these things ASAP. You are doing yourself a disservice and you will find yourself the subject of a bar complaint. Always put the best you forward and remember your reputation is all you have so protect it at all times.

22ND LAW
OF
FORECLOSURE
DEFENSE

FORECLOSURE DEFENSE
LAW
22

Learn About Securitization Failure

This play's in tune with knowing the life of your loan. Most loans before 2007 are loans originated and sold in the secondary markets. This is a Wall Street term that's kind of like backroom gambling. These loans were securitized into pools of loans broken into tranches within vehicles known as Real Estate Mortgage Investment Conduits (REMIC) Trusts. Sounds complicated? It is.

Often times, the securitization of loans failed because the loan notes were never transferred into the securitization trust by the closing date identified in the Pooling and Servicing Agreement ("PSA"). Understanding securitization failure is important to realizing not only how to argue the defective positions of a foreclosing plaintiffs standing, it will also help you filter out the land mines and brick walls you will run into under securitization conspiracy theories. Remember, you always have to keep your arguments specific to your case and your case only.

Most attorneys suffer failure when arguing the securitization of loans. This is because they address securitization from the wrong angle. Consider a plaintiff that is trustee for a trust and the PSA identifies all of the parties to the transfer of the note and mortgage. Now consider the endorsements on the note and the chain of assignment of mortgages in public records. Often times, they won't match the PSA securitization chain. You have just confirmed one of many lies.

Securitization itself, stems from money lent by investors believing they were investing in loans already purchased, but never knew the money invested was funding the purchase of the loans. Learn securitization and the lies become clear.

23RD LAW
OF
FORECLOSURE
DEFENSE

FORECLOSURE DEFENSE

LAW

23

Consider the Position That You Are Sitting at a Table of Thieves

Without creating offense, consider all the players of this potential unlawful foreclosure action to the likes of sitting at a table of thieves. This includes you too.

The party that hired the law firm to sue in someone else's name, is seeking financial gain using someone else because in their own name, they would be unsuccessful. Now take the foreclosure mill law firm who knows that the party, whose name they are suing on, is not the party that hired them. They've never even spoken with them yet; they will take that retainer money and spin the fraud while protecting themselves in litigation privilege.

Then there is the judge that received a raise to move these foreclosure cases along to closure to clear their dockets. Sometimes their investments or retirement funds are intertwined with foreclosing party. These judges' rule in favor of the foreclosing party despite conflicts of interest and will prevent you from succeeding.

Lastly, here you are defending and/or suing to win with years of no mortgage payments made. Thus, you are sitting at a table of thieves because everyone at the table is looking to deprive the other of financial gain to their own detriment. That may sound offensive but toughen up and act as if because if you don't, you will be the losing party at this gambling table where everyone is putting up money to win the big prize.

24TH LAW
OF
FORECLOSURE
DEFENSE

FORECLOSURE DEFENSE
LAW
24

Document Everything the Moment it Happens

Don't wait until you get back home or back to your office to write your notes about what took place in a hearing, a conversation you just had about the case or something interesting you heard the other party mention. Get it all down when it happens.

This is 2020. You don't have to write it down, you can speak your notes now. They designed your smartphone to make things easy for you. Use one of the many audio applications on your phone to repeat what was just said and translate it when you have the opportunity. Failing to record the information causes a lapse in memory or causes you to recite the information different than how it was first stated.

It is also important that you not wait until later to put a scheduled hearing in your calendar, do it the moment you find out. Set several alert's days out that lead up to the hearing so you are aware a hearing is coming up. Make sure you give yourself enough time to get things done that have scheduled deadlines.

Taking audio notes is good practice and keeps you on point in your case. Remember, the court is bias against you. If you fail to appear, the judge will rule against you.

25TH LAW OF FORECLOSURE DEFENSE

FORECLOSURE DEFENSE
LAW
25

Always Digitize Your Documents

I will say it again, this is 2020. Paper often gets ruined, misplaced or destroyed. Store enough paper and you'll throw it out with spring cleaning. Invest in a good quality scanner, one that has a document feeder that can scan up to 30 pages a minute. Color copy capability doesn't hurt too.

Scan your mortgage statements and ANY correspondence you receive related to your loan. Save them on to a dedicated external drive. You can even back them up to the cloud so you can have access to them on your smart phone or tablet. The point is, one day you will need to produce them, and you want to have them accessible and ready to print or produce.

In addition, always scan at a document level, not a page level. Make sure you always save each document as a PDF file at the 300 DPI setting and ensure each page is OCR'd (Optical Character Recognition) for easy text or phrase searching. This way, if you ever need to find something specific, a quick search in the toolbar will pull up every document that contains your keyword search or phrase.

Lastly, purchase a sizable external hard drive that holds all of your case data on it. Some people like to save everything on their main computer hard drive. I do not recommend this. Computers have a way of dying and you don't want your case files destroyed. Using an external drive keeps it safe. It also allows you to unplug it and take it with you anywhere your laptop goes. This is great when you want to spend a few hours at Starbucks getting some work done.

26TH LAW
OF
FORECLOSURE
DEFENSE

FORECLOSURE DEFENSE

LAW

26

Take Up Things That Teach You How to Control Your Stress

Foreclosure is stressful. Couples have gotten divorced over it. Entire families have been destroyed over it. Children have lost the safety and security they developed in having their bedrooms and the stability of a home. People have committed suicide and elderly homeowners have watched their spouses die only to be left alone in this life.

Take up anything that will help you release stress. Change your diet to a healthier lifestyle. Go to the gym and engage in cardio, exercise or take up yoga. Listen to Zen like music during your day if you can. Spend at least 30 minutes of your day in meditation or prayer to relax your mind and find peace within yourself. Don't allow the unknowns in foreclosure create stress and adversity in your life.

Remember, stress causes severe mental and physical harm. It will affect you if you let it so don't. Use the adversity of foreclosure to make positive life changes. If you ever found yourself to be a procrastinator, now is the time to become proactive. Use this negative event in your life to create positive change in your life and in the lives of those you love most.

Most importantly, recognize the frustrations foreclosure brings. Don't create insecurity or reasons to argue and fight with your spouse and children. Be mindful. Be smart. Show your family more love than ever before. There is great strength in numbers. Don't let foreclosure divide and conquer you.

27TH LAW
OF
FORECLOSURE
DEFENSE

FORECLOSURE DEFENSE

LAW
27

Prepare Yourself and Your Family for Life Changes

One of the biggest mistakes people make when faced with foreclosure is, they wait until it's too late. Don't be one of those people. You have options, you just don't know it. This book is a huge resource because it not only makes you mindful of the things you need to consider when facing an unlawful foreclosure, it also gives you information and direction on how to help you fight.

There are very few foreclosure consultants let alone qualified ones who can educate you on your options. No matter the option you choose, when you're served with those foreclosure papers, the clock begins so, prepare yourself and your family for these life changes. It can be very stressful but can also be rewarding. It's up to you if your preparation is positive or negative. Negativity solves nothing but being smart and positive will turn this negative foreclosure situation into a positive one.

The best way to prepare is to detach the emotional side from the realistic financial side. Your property may not be worth what it was when you purchased it. It may be worth much more than what you owe and has a surplus which means if the property is sold, you may get the amount that is left over and greater than the judgment amount. No matter the circumstances, remove the emotion and you will see the financial benefits and harms so you can think and move accordingly.

28TH LAW OF FORECLOSURE DEFENSE

FORECLOSURE DEFENSE
LAW
28

Don't Let Anyone or Anything Intimidate You

If you haven't figured it out yet by the time you've gotten to this 28th Law, let me say it outright and clear for you to understand like an old Michael Jackson song: you are not alone... I am here for you!

Never let any of these legal documents, attorneys, judges or fraudsters intimidate you. I am your big red nuclear button. If you're a homeowner, you can call on me to jump in and stand in your shoes to direct your attorney or hire a good one for you. I am your autopilot. I have no problem coming in and quarterbacking your case for you.

If you are a practicing attorney that doesn't know how to proceed or just needs help, general or specific, I am always available to ensure you have all the tools and resources at your fingertips to litigate an unlawful foreclosure case to success.

Sometimes in life, we need to put our pride aside and reach out for help. You have access to the #1 Foreclosure Defense Litigation Consultant and Expert at your complete disposal.

29TH LAW OF FORECLOSURE DEFENSE

FORECLOSURE DEFENSE
LAW
29

Don't Be Afraid of Your Adversary Make Them Afraid of You

Some lawyers like being overly aggressive and intimidating. Often deliberately being an ass or a jerk. Maybe its compensation for their lacking or maybe they are naturally rude and obnoxious. Whatever the reason, don't let it affect you the way they intended. More importantly, you don't have to be an asshole to deal with one.

Be like boiling water, change form and rise above it. Always meet them with kindness but the assertive, intelligent and direct kind that always makes them feel smaller when they leave your presence. Never be afraid to be direct and to the point. Never beat around the bush, never misrepresent the facts and never be like them.

Don't confuse their assertive way with professionalism. It's not professional to lie. It's not professional to be an officer of the court and sell your soul for a paycheck. Unlawful foreclosure is a crime and anyone who helps the fraudsters are aiding and abetting criminals engaged in a criminal act.

Remember that they are trying to take your home away from you. When you have factually determined fraud, don't be afraid to say FRAUD! Call them out when you have a smoking gun document at every turn. When a lawyer lies in court and you can factually refute it, don't be scared to say to the court, it's a shame counsel just lied to this court and deliberately misrepresented the facts.

When you respectfully, professionally and directly, call out your adversaries, you get the courts attention. Just make sure you're right each time you do.

30TH LAW OF FORECLOSURE DEFENSE

FORECLOSURE DEFENSE
LAW
30

Prepare for War

When war is imminent, it is imperative that you prepare and stock up your war chest. Remember that we cannot win a war without financing. Whether you're pro-se or not, don't make the mistake of failing to fund your war chest.

The best way to do this is by remembering you had a mortgage payment. Even though the bank won't accept it anymore, put the full amount, or as close to that amount, to the side to finance your war. Be strategic in how you finance your war, so you have financial reserves for each of your battles such as filing fees for counterclaims, deposition fees, transcript costs and appeals if they become necessary.

Another method to consider when reviewing your options to finance your war is renting out your property during the duration of the foreclosure battles. Consider that your occupation of the property does not generate revenue but by renting it for the duration of the foreclosure, you've turned a negative situation into a positive one. Renting gives you residual income that can allow you to finance your war, add additional income to your current income and detaches you from the emotional strain of having to leave your property on someone else's terms should you lose.

Lastly, war has casualties and consequences. You have to take the good with the bad, the sweet with the sour. You will lose some battles, but you cannot be discouraged. Know that and accept it. Remember that we learn best when we fail so when you fail, make a conscious effort to learn from it.

31ST LAW
OF
FORECLOSURE
DEFENSE

FORECLOSURE DEFENSE
LAW
31

Even Though a Foreclosure Complaint was Filed Against You, Assume Everything in the Complaint is a Lie

Just because you're being sued doesn't mean the truth is being told. Remember, this is a foreclosure designed to sell your home and make hundreds of thousands of dollars. Replicate that on a scale in the millions and you have a trillion-dollar industry. If you think it's all about the truth, you're fooling yourself.

As the saying goes, the devil is in the details. Begin your defense preparations by addressing the details in every allegation of the complaint. Validate the truthfulness of that allegation. Every time you find a contradiction or a discrepancy, deep dive into it and find the reason why.

For example, you may see an allegation that the interest in the note and mortgage was transferred via an Assignment of Mortgage attached as an exhibit to the complaint. When you review the assignment of mortgage you find it's from Mortgage Electronic Registrations Systems ("MERS") as nominee for the original lender who when out of business in 2008 however the assignment is dated 2016. There is a falsity here. Don't leave it at that. Do a deep dive background into the closing of the business in 2008. Show how it was legally impossible for MERS to act on behalf of a company that no longer exists. Tie that to the fact that MERS memorialized this falsity and then recorded it in public records which is a crime.

Dismantling the details in the complaint begins the process of helping the court understand what's really in front of them.

32ND LAW
OF
FORECLOSURE
DEFENSE

FORECLOSURE DEFENSE
LAW
32

Be Honest with Yourself About What You Want to Achieve

Foreclosure is emotional and very draining. Once you're caught in the foreclosure web, the only way out is a permanent loan modification or taking steps to ensure a satisfaction of the mortgage is achieved. A dismissal of a foreclosure case will only prompt another filing and if you keep getting the case dismissed, you can expect to keep watching the bank refile.

Be honest about your goal. If your goal is to stay in the property until you can save up enough money to move to a new property, then let that be the goal. One of the biggest mistakes attorneys and borrowers make is not being honest about what the client wants to achieve. Even worst, most attorneys don't know how to achieve what a client wants. This is why choosing the right attorney is so critical.

Communication is the key and if you communicate honestly about what you want or as an attorney, what you believe you can achieve, the attorney client relationship will be better served. Being honest about what you want to achieve will get you what you want. Regardless of the desire, albeit a loan modification, a cash for keys, to fight for a dismissal or counter-sue for fraud, flush it out up front and direct your goal.

33RD LAW
OF
FORECLOSURE
DEFENSE

FORECLOSURE DEFENSE LAW

33

Understanding Offensive and Defensive Strategies

Don't wing it. In this world there is trained and untrained. Get trained! Don't be a mediocre foreclosure defense attorney. Perfect your craft. Be the best foreclosure defense attorney out there. If you have to remain pro-se, read, learn, learn some more and apply.

Amazingly, despite the entire country going into foreclosure most people cannot name 10 foreclosure defense attorneys. Don't be an uneducated client. Imagine a boxing match between a trained boxer and an untrained opponent. You can hope for a haymaker, but you will probably lose and lose bad.

Be prepared by creating an offensive and defensive strategy and then execute it methodically. Understand what is available to you as an option offensively and what is available as an option defensively. Remember that the best defense is a good offense and a good offense creates leverage.

For example, if all you are trying to do is buy time to save up enough money to move then filing a counterclaim wouldn't be necessary. But if you were trying to void out certain documents believed to have been created in fraud and you're trying to get a satisfaction of the mortgage, a counterclaim and/or cross complaint may create the leverage you need to achieve that goal.

34TH LAW OF FORECLOSURE DEFENSE

FORECLOSURE DEFENSE

LAW

34

Always Assume the Court is Pro-Bank and Anti-Homeowner So Act Accordingly

At some point in the case, albeit in a pleading filed by the Plaintiff or in a hearing at court, you will hear them say something like, "the Defendant hasn't made a mortgage payment on this loan for X amount of years judge". This is the classic prejudicial statement made to the court to ensure the judge always maintains a bias toward you. So, while the fraudster attempting to foreclose is trying to convince the court you're a deadbeat, consider responding artfully. Those comments might hold weight if the foreclosing party was someone that was actually damaged by non-payment, but they're not that party.

Remember that a default occurs when a payment was not received. A default does not occur because you weren't the one to make the payment directly. That may sound like splitting hairs, but it isn't. The full payment of the loan via a third party of any kind is payment received that must be applied. Just because it was not you that made the payment, does not mean a payment was not received by them via another party. For example, if insurance paid off the entire debt or some other third party means did, no default has occurred.

Also consider mirror lending. What if you closed on a loan that required a monthly mortgage payment of $2,000.00 per month to the named lender on your loan, who in turn, owed a monthly payment amount of $500 a month to the undisclosed funding source (investor)? Consider you were lied to from the very beginning and don't know all the facts. So was the judge. So was America.

35TH LAW OF FORECLOSURE DEFENSE

FORECLOSURE DEFENSE
LAW
35

You Are Likely Not in Default and Most Certainly Are Not a Deadbeat

Sometimes the court needs to be educated that if there's a default, then there's a charge off. Charge offs are not rocket science. Remember, a default on a loan is 99% the product of a charge off. A charge off means it has left the books of the party you actually owe, an insurance claim filed and an insurance payment of the loan amount (if not more), has been paid in full.

Whoever is foreclosing has not been damaged by your so-called non-payment. Remind the court that a party has to suffer damages to sue. When you can sway the court to pay attention to who this foreclosure fraudster is and how much they paid to be here, you will see them tell the court they don't have to show how much they paid for the loan.

You will never see these bottom feeders try to claim that amount in their final judgment figures either. A good defender has the task of convincing the court the foreclosing party is a sham, a thief who has no legal entitlement to bring this foreclosure action and have judgment entered in their favor.

In new, refiled foreclosure cases, the default alleged is likely a default date erroneously created while the previous foreclosure action was active. How could a new default exist when the full balance of the loan was already in active acceleration? How can a default letter be provided years after the alleged default? Be vigorous in educating the court that this kind of default is not the product of non-payment but rather, is the product of pure fiction and fabrication by the opposition.

36TH LAW
OF
FORECLOSURE
DEFENSE

FORECLOSURE DEFENSE LAW

36

Even if the Foreclosure Mill Law Firm Prosecuting You Doesn't Respect the Law You Should

As layman to the law, we hold the law in high regards. We believe that the law will always prevail and so if the law is on your side, then you should prevail. There is, or at least was, good reason to believe this. The judiciary system by design was supposed to ensure that if the law was on your side, then you would likely be the prevailing party.

To ensure this, the law provides that whether an attorney was prosecuting or defending a case, the same oath and rules of conduct held both as officers of the court first. Next was the judge who was also bound by oath and rules of conduct. Their job was to remain impartial and adjudicate cases on the merits.

In unlawful foreclosure cases, you will find that foreclosure mill law firms break their oaths and don't follow the rules of conduct. You will always find that judges rarely remain impartial and adjudicate cases on the merits. If you find it offensive, know that most of America is just as disappointed as you.

Their actions don't justify you to become unprofessional and disrespect the law. Often times, showing integrity and honor where it is lacking, reminds the room of its importance and value. Where there is darkness, be the light. Even if you lose you win.

37TH LAW
OF
FORECLOSURE
DEFENSE

FORECLOSURE DEFENSE LAW

37

The Difference Between Foreclosure Practice and Theories

Just because a lawyer has a law degree and a license to practice law, doesn't mean they're good litigators. A therapist with a strong academic background in parenting who doesn't have children, lacks a certain level of personal experience only a mother or father can advise or understand. The point is, there is a difference between experience versus argumentative theories.

In foreclosure, they saturate the internet with foreclosure theories on how to defend a foreclosure. Given most foreclosures are

110

unlawful for a variety of reasons, these defense theories are almost always premised on information that is not specific to your loan or your case. It is important to understand that arguments that suggest you are the victim of an incredible conspiracy, even though true, will fall upon deaf ears.

Sound foreclosure defense and litigation defense overall requires that you stick to the facts of your case only. Believe that there is enough false information hidden throughout your case that you can use, without referencing the greater conspiracy against the American dream.

38TH LAW
OF
FORECLOSURE
DEFENSE

FORECLOSURE DEFENSE
LAW
38

Stay Away from Sovereign Citizen Arguments

Let's be clear about the "I'm a sovereign citizen, this court doesn't have any jurisdiction over me" position. It doesn't work. As a sovereign citizen, you can protect your property from unlawful trespass, inclusive of government agencies without a warrant. You may own the property but not own the land or you my own the land and the property on it. Regardless of the argument, many people confuse the sovereign citizen angle as effective because it's delaying the foreclosure for several years. It's not the sovereign citizen claim that's delaying it, it's the plethora of motion filings that is.

Every time a motion is filed, it has to be heard. For it to be heard, it must be set on the courts calendar. The foreclosure epidemic caused the inundation of the court's dockets with motions and hearings. So, the court could schedule a hearing many months out before it's heard. File 10 or 15 different irrelevant motions that will probably get denied and you have years of delays.

The fact is, these voluminous motions and arguments don't work and are frowned upon. What they accomplished in a majority of jurisdictions was for courts across the country to change their local rules to require motions that were not evidentiary in nature, do not require a hearing. Stated another way, now judges get to rule on a motion without a hearing, to expedite the judicial process.

39THLAW OF FORECLOSURE DEFENSE

FORECLOSURE DEFENSE

LAW

39

What is Mortgage Electronic Registration Systems ("MERS") and How Does it Affect You

The 2008 housing market crash had many veins to the heart of the reason. What is important to understand is that money moves fast. It moves electronically. It doesn't move by someone writing a check, placing it in a FedEx envelope and overnighting it. What if you had to do that for every loan that is closed?

When Wall Street conspirers packaged these loans, they needed the documents to move as fast as the money. So, if the money moved electronically, the documents needed to move electronically too. Enter MERS. When a closing agent had a homeowner sign all the documents, the original documents were to be scanned and uploaded to into MERS. The original documents were then destroyed (according to the Florida Banking Association and everyone else on the topic).

MERS allowed for the documents and any legal assignment, transfer or conveyance of the loan to occur. But it was mishandled and abused. Foreclosure Mill Law Firms used their own employees and notaries to falsely identify themselves as officers of MERS and create Assignment of Mortgages solely for foreclosure litigation to memorialize events that never happened and if they did, didn't happen timely and was void.

Where a foreclosure involves MERS, you must deep dive the facts because there is a good chance your case involves falsities asserted to create standing to foreclose where none exists.

40TH LAW OF FORECLOSURE DEFENSE

FORECLOSURE DEFENSE

LAW

40

Robo-Signed Documents and Recording False Information in Public Records

Robo-signing is a phrase used in the foreclosure arena that means the signature that appears, was put there by someone other than the actual person. This is done by someone using a rubberstamp of a person's signature or just flat out signing that person's name as if they had done it themselves.

In the context of a robo-signed document, they (the fraudsters) would argue the authorized signatory gave permission to allow others to sign their name because the volume of documents dictated the use of a rubberstamp or other's signing their name. We (foreclosure defenders) would argue hogwash! Fraud is fraud! The use or the systematic use of someone else's signature without their knowledge, especially years after they stopped working for the company, is fraud.

Creating a document that memorializes a transaction that never occurred and have it robo-signed by people claiming to be officers of a company they never worked for, is more than a falsity, it is fraudulent behavior, when it is in furtherance of stealing your home. When that kind of document is recorded in public records to deceive the public, you and the court to rely on it, is a crime and is subject to civil remedy.

41ST LAW
OF
FORECLOSURE
DEFENSE

FORECLOSURE DEFENSE LAW

41

Understanding the Robo-Witness and the Purpose of Their Robo-Testimony

As the courts and legislatures began implementing new rules, laws and requirements prior to the filing of a foreclosure action by a fraudster, the use of robo-signed documents in foreclosure cases have become more difficult to use. As a result, America was introduced to foreclosure 2.0, the "Robo-Witness".

A Robo-Witness is a person who has no personal knowledge about a loan but will get up on the stand, under oath and swear they do, under what they call the business records exception rule. You see, for purposes of evidence and testimony, the person testifying about a particular document, is that they must have first-hand knowledge - personal knowledge. Usually this would mean the person created the document, was a party to the document or had some kind of specialized relationship to the document. That person would then be qualified to get up on the stand and talk about the document. Without this qualification, the witness's testimony would be deemed hearsay.

To get around hearsay, Robo-Witnesses and their employers (the fraudsters), rely on the business records exception rule. This rule allows for documents to be introduced into evidence as long as the person testifying about them is "qualified" under the rule except "qualified" is not defined by the law or case law so, it's subject to the interpretation of the court who is predominately pro-fraudster.

42ND LAW
OF
FORECLOSURE
DEFENSE

FORECLOSURE DEFENSE
LAW
42

Why They Circumvent Hearsay with the Business Records Exception Rule

The short answer is because they have no personal knowledge. The records they intend to present as evidence at trial are documents they created for the sole purpose of litigation and they need a way to get them in. The business record exception rule is the new "go to".

In most unlawful foreclosure actions, the named Plaintiff is not the party that hired the foreclosure mill law firm to sue. It was someone claiming to be the servicer for them. In conjunction with that effort, the servicer claims to be the holder of the business records for the named Plaintiff. When trial comes, the servicer will produce what they call a corporate witness who has no personal knowledge and will help the foreclosure mill attorney try to introduce evidence under the business record exception.

Under this rule, the fraudsters are required to establish the record was made at or near the time of the event; was made by or from information transmitted by a person with knowledge; was kept in the ordinary course of a regularly conducted business activity; and that it was a regular practice of that business to make such a record.

They created all of these records for the sole purpose of foreclosure litigation with one pursuit in sight which is to get a judgment, sell the home and take the money. Non-Jury trials begin and end with this witness. If they get the records in under the rule, you're pretty much done and will lose your home.

43RD LAW
OF
FORECLOSURE
DEFENSE

FORECLOSURE DEFENSE
LAW
43

The Power of a Loan Modification in an Unlawful Foreclosure Action

Unlawful foreclosure means a party that was never damaged and has no legal right to sue, has opted to file a fraudulent lawsuit to steal your property. Unlawful foreclosure shows its ugly head through the filing of misleading and fraudulent documents in public records to deceive the public, you and the court. It's usually a foreclosure filed by someone down a long chain of bogus servicing transfers versus actual bona fide sales of the actual loan.

The initial fraud is hidden by ensuring multiple transfers like a game of Three Card Monty so that in the end, everyone believes the fraudster foreclosing, is actually legally entitled to. Use this to your advantage.

Loan modification efforts can force a new legal document in furtherance of the fraud. In that loan modification document, you will probably find the real culprit of the fraud identifying themselves, for the first time, as the "lender" when you know they've lent nothing... ever! They want to use this newly created legal document to erase all the fraudulent ambiguity in the documents of the past. Use the loan modification to pull them out of the darkness. You will see this fact immediately when a loan modification is offered to you, that names one party as the lender, while another party is named as the Plaintiff in the foreclosure. Ask the question in reverse: why isn't the named Plaintiff in the foreclosure identified as the lender in the loan modification documents? There is power in a loan modification. This is why the fraudsters try to require you to sign a settlement agreement that waives their fraud.

44TH LAW OF FORECLOSURE DEFENSE

FORECLOSURE DEFENSE
LAW
44

The Power of a Cash for Keys Offer in an Unlawful Foreclosure Action

If you ever want to see your fraudsters hand, throw out a potential settlement offer in good faith, for a cash for keys. See if they will entertain an offer that is a minimum of 12 months of aggregated mortgage payments. If they consider the ballpark, then you might want to consider how 10 months or so of payments could help you if you wanted to take advantage of it and move on into your next home.

Cash for keys can also feel insulting. Fraudsters often offer nothing except an extended sale date in exchange for your consent to judgment. After a judgment has been entered, if you are still filing motions that delay the process for them to get title and a writ of possession, they may offer you $1,500 to $3,500 as a cash for keys to expedite your removal and ensure you don't destroy the property.

Cash for key offers are helpful in educating you in how to proceed against them. It's also a great way to gauge how they are thinking in the case. Getting a cash for keys offer out there in the beginning will never hurt you. Remember always start high. If you are hurting them in the case, you may see a larger than usual offer. If you're losing, you may see less.

45TH LAW OF FORECLOSURE DEFENSE

FORECLOSURE DEFENSE

LAW

45

Foreclosure May Be the End of One Thing and the Beginning of Another

Consider staying in peace. Positive Education Always Creates Elevation (PEACE). Foreclosure creates opportunity because it creates a pressure to act.

Immediately, foreclosure brings a panic that makes you believe you are out of time and you're about to lose. A fast-tracked case that goes undefended can end in as quick as eight months, however, a properly defended foreclosure action can take up a minimum of 3 years and go past 5 years.

Positive education in foreclosure allows you to slow down time like the matrix. It allows you to create elevation and see the whole playing field. Educating yourself in foreclosure defense stimulates your mind, raises your intellect and most times, causes you to think differently overall about life, family, finances, politics and so much more.

Foreclosure has a way of awakening your soul and spirituality about the evil that men do as well as the good. That may sound a bit drastic, but people don't really understand the power of a quarter or half million dollars in the air. People have robbed and killed for much less. Don't take it likely.

You will find that at the end of this foreclosure journey, should you engage it wholeheartedly with both eyes wide open, you'll no longer be the same person. That doesn't have to be a bad thing and you should consciously make it a good one – win, lose or draw.

46TH LAW
OF
FORECLOSURE
DEFENSE

FORECLOSURE DEFENSE

LAW

46

Judicial States vs. Non-Judicial States and Unlawful Foreclosure

Judicial states require a foreclosure lawsuit be filed against you. A judgment must then be entered, a sale conducted, certificate of title changed, and a writ of possession issued. Once that is all done, the sheriff can then post a 3-day notice on your door warning you they will come change the locks and take possession of the property. If you don't have your belongings out by the time they come, they will have it removed and put on the front lawn by the gutter.

In a Non-Judicial state, the fraudsters only provide a Notice of Sale to give you notice that they will sell your property on the courthouse steps on a specific date. To prevent this, it is you that must file a lawsuit against them and seek court intervention to restrain them from conducting the sale. What is important to remember in a non-judicial state is that you cannot bring an unlawful foreclosure action if you have not been unlawfully foreclosed. This means the sale had occurred already.

No matter judicial or non-judicial, unlawful foreclosure means the party trying to steal your home has systematically created misleading and fraudulent documents to create standing where it doesn't exist, for the sole purpose of stealing your home. While the arguments may be the same in judicial and non-judicial states, the rules of civil procedure and evidence differ. Learn them well. Also, identify the state statutes that cover the recording of false statements and/or documents in public records. Crimes committed that have civil remedies to them, play a critical role in holding these fraudsters feet to the fire.

47TH LAW OF FORECLOSURE DEFENSE

FORECLOSURE DEFENSE
LAW
47

Consider Your Financial Options in Foreclosure

You've made 5 years of payments in the amount of $2,500 a month for a total of $150,000. You're being unlawfully foreclosed and stand to lose all the money you put in and the house and the house itself. What do you do?

Consider a reverse financial move as an option wherein you rent out your home for the duration of the litigation for the current market rental value of the property. This can be significantly beneficial in several ways.

A well-contested foreclosure can last a minimum of 3 years. If you rented out your property for the duration of those three years at $2,500, you would make back $90,000. Sure, it's not all the money you put in but it's a significant amount.

Another benefit to renting out the property during the duration of the foreclosure is, not only do you now have residual monthly income, you slowly become emotionally detached from the stress of potentially losing the property. By renting, you are in effect, moving on and forward.

Lastly, consider that if you win the foreclosure, you can continue to rent the property or move back in. These financial options should not be ignored. Those that take advantage of these financial options tend to be more objective in the defense of the unlawful foreclosure.

48TH LAW OF FORECLOSURE DEFENSE

FORECLOSURE DEFENSE
LAW
48

Purchase My Next Book
The Art of Foreclosure Defense

After the release of the 48 Laws of Foreclosure Defense will come the Art of Foreclosure Defense – Unlawful Foreclosure in 2020. Obviously, this is self-promotion however, I designed the 48 Laws of Foreclosure to bring your attention to 48 crucial topics you should be aware of in an unlawful foreclosure action. The Art of Foreclosure Defense gives attorneys and pro-se defendants the details of all the strategies and tactics I teach attorneys to use, to defend an unlawful foreclosure.

The book identifies every step in the litigation process, proper defenses, counterclaims and who to crossclaim. It has an in-depth focus on discovery requests, depositions, and tactics that force your opposition out of their comfort zone.

Among other important topics, the book goes deep into how to cross-examine the fraudsters corporate witness on a level that not only establishes the witness is not "qualified" under the business record exception rule, it attacks the information "boarding process" and establishes its unreliability. The book explains in great depth how to exclude electronically created documents presented as exhibits and sure-fire ways to ensure the foreclosing fraudster fail to meet their burden.

A successful defense of an unlawful foreclosure lawsuit is won by getting all of the most critical information because, he who has the most knowledge, wins!

Made in the USA
Monee, IL
15 October 2021